Great White Sharks

ABDO
Publishing Company
A Buddy Book
by
Julie Murray

VISIT US AT
www.abdopub.com

Published by Buddy Books, an imprint of ABDO Publishing Company, 4940 Viking Drive, Suite 622, Edina, Minnesota 55435. Copyright © 2003 by Abdo Consulting Group, Inc. International copyrights reserved in all countries. No part of this book may be reproduced in any form without written permission from the publisher.

Printed in the United States.

Edited by: Christy DeVillier
Contributing Editors: Matt Ray, Michael P. Goecke
Graphic Design: Maria Hosley
Image Research: Deborah Coldiron
Cover Photograph: Fotosearch
Interior Photographs: Fotosearch, Minden Pictures, Getty Images

Library of Congress Cataloging-in-Publication Data

Murray, Julie, 1969-
  Great white sharks/Julie Murray.
      p. cm. — (Animal kingdom)
  Summary: An introduction to the habitat, physical characteristics, and behavior of the white shark.
  ISBN 1-57765-706-3
      1. White shark—Juvenile literature. [1. White shark. 2. Sharks.] I. Title. II. Animal
  kingdom (Edina, Minn.)

QL638.95.L3 M87 2002
597.3'3—dc21

2001053546

Contents

Sharks

Sharks have been around for more than 300 million years. These fish have been around since the days of the dinosaurs. Today, there are more than 350 kinds of sharks.

This southern stingray has cartilage instead of bones.

There are fish with bones and fish with **cartilage**. Cartilage is softer than bone. It is bendable and lightweight. Sharks have cartilage instead of bones. Other fish with cartilage are skates and rays.

Great White Sharks

    Of all fish, great white sharks are the largest **predators**. Other sea animals have to watch out for this mighty hunter. Strong and deadly, the great white shark can crush bones.

It is safer to study great whites from inside a cage.

Why do some people call the great white shark "man eater" or "white death"? Some people believe these sharks hunt people. It is true that hungry sharks sometimes bite people. Sharks bite when they are scared, too. However, people are not natural **prey** for sharks.

Sandpaper Skin

Sharks do not have scales like most fish. Instead, sharks have tiny "skin teeth." These "skin teeth" are called **denticles**. Denticles make the great white's skin rough and tough. It is very hard for other animals to bite through a shark's tough skin.

What They Look Like

Great white sharks can grow as long as 20 feet (6 m). Some great whites weigh as much as 5,000 pounds (2,268 kg). Female great white sharks grow to become bigger than males.

The great white shark is not white all over. Their backs can be gray, blue, or black. Their bellies are white or cream-colored. These colors make it harder to see these sharks in the water.

The great white's coloring matches the water.

Dorsal fin

Pectoral
fins

The great white shark has a strong
tail and **fins** for swimming. The big fin
on a shark's back is its dorsal fin. The
pectoral fins are the two front fins. Fins
help sharks steer themselves.

Where They Live

Great white sharks live all over the world. They live near the coasts of all **continents** except Antarctica. They live around Hawaii and other ocean islands, too. These sharks commonly stay near the ocean's surface.

Home of the
Great White Shark

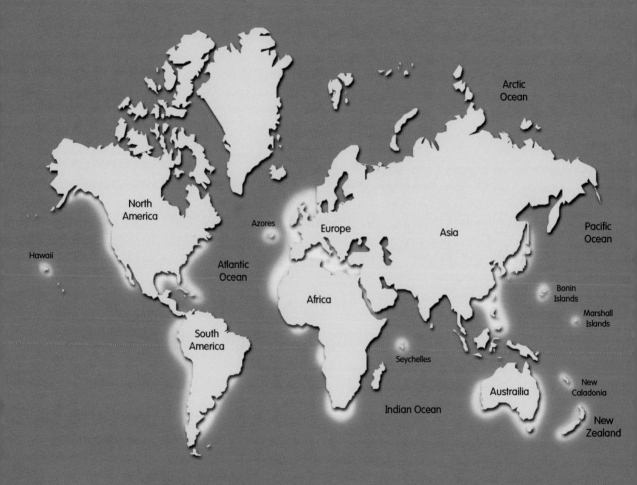

Arctic
Ocean

North
America

Azores

Europe

Asia

Pacific
Ocean

Hawaii

Atlantic
Ocean

Africa

Bonin
Islands

Marshall
Islands

South
America

Seychelles

Austrailia

New
Caladonia

Indian Ocean

New
Zealand

 Where Great White
Sharks Live

Hunting And Eating

Great white sharks are meat-eaters. They often go after **prey** that looks old, sick, or hurt. They hunt sea lions, seals, dolphins, squid, turtles, and other sharks. Great whites will eat many kinds of ocean fish, too.

Great white sharks hunt during the day. Some sharks hunt at sunrise or sunset. The great white's coloring, or **camouflage**, helps it sneak up behind **prey**. These **predators** may not kill their prey right away. After a bite or two, the shark may leave and wait for its prey to die.

Other animals must watch out for the mighty great white.

A Sixth Sense

Sharks have the same five senses as people. These five senses are: sight, smell, touch, taste, and hearing. Unlike people, sharks can also sense **electricity**. All animals have an electric field around them. So, great whites can use this sixth sense to find **prey**.

Sharks use their sense of electricity to find food.

Deadly Teeth

Inside a shark's mouth are many rows of triangle-shaped teeth. Some of the great white's teeth are over two inches (five cm) long. Each tooth has tiny, sharp points along each side. The shark's sharp teeth can cut very well.

The great white may lose about 1,000
teeth in its lifetime. When a shark's
tooth falls out, another tooth takes its
place. Sharks are the only animals that
replace their teeth in this way.

Shark Pups

Baby great white sharks begin life inside eggs. These eggs are inside the mother shark. After hatching, the baby sharks stay inside the mother and grow bigger.

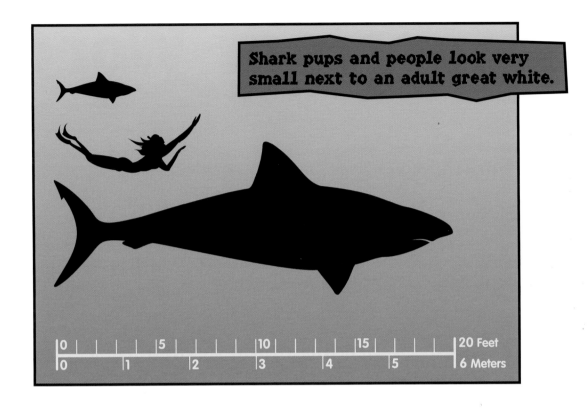

Shark pups and people look very small next to an adult great white.

| 0 | | | | 5 | | | | 10 | | | | 15 | | | | 20 Feet |
| 0 | | 1 | | 2 | | 3 | | 4 | | 5 | | 6 Meters |

Great whites have a few babies at a time. Newborn great whites, or pups, are about four feet (one m) long. They can swim and hunt right away. So, great white pups can leave their mothers right after birth.

Important Words

camouflage when an animal's coloring matches what is around it. Camouflage helps animals stay hidden from others.

cartilage matter that is tough and bendable. Cartilage is in a person's nose and ears.

continent one of the seven largest land masses on earth.

denticles a shark's "skin teeth."

electricity something that happens in nature. Lightning is one form of electricity.

fins flat body parts of fish used for swimming and steering.

predator an animal that hunts and eats other animals.

prey an animal that is food for another animal.

Web Sites

Great White Shark

www.enchantedlearning.com/subjects/sharks/species/Greatwhite.shtml
This web site features information on the great white and many other sharks.

Sharks and Their Relatives

www.seaworld.org/infobooks/Sharks&Rays/home.html
Learn more about many kinds of sharks.

Shark Surfari!

www.nationalgeographic.com/features/97/sharks
This special site for kids features facts, pictures, a quiz, and links to other fun shark web sites.

Index